Easy Vegetarian Foods

From Around the World

Sheila Griffin Llanas

E Enslow Elementary

Library of Congress Cataloging-in-Publication Data

Llanas, Sheila Griffin, 1958-
 Easy vegetarian foods from around the world / Sheila Griffin Llanas.
   p. cm. — (Easy cookbooks for kids)
 Includes bibliographical references and index.
 Summary: "Make simple vegetarian foods from countries around the world"
—Provided by publisher.
 ISBN 978-0-7660-3764-9
 1. Vegetarian cooking—Juvenile literature. 2. International cooking—Juvenile
literature. 3. Quick and easy cooking—Juvenile literature. 4. Cookbooks. I. Title.
 TX837.L535 2011
 641.5'636—dc22
                              2010047605

Paperback ISBN 978-1-59845-271-6

Printed in China
052011 Leo Paper Group, Heshan City, Guangdong, China
10 9 8 7 6 5 4 3 2 1

To Our Readers: We have done our best to make sure all Internet addresses in this book were active and appropriate when we went to press. However, the author and the publisher have no control over and assume no liability for the material available on those Internet sites or on other Web sites they may link to. Any comments or suggestions can be sent by e-mail to comments@enslow.com or to the address on the back cover.

Every effort has been made to locate all copyright holders of material used in this book. If any errors or omissions have occurred, corrections will be made in future editions of this book.

Illustration Credits: All photos are from Shutterstock.com except as noted.
© 2011 Photos.com/ © Chris Scredon (tofu and vegetables), p. 17; ©1999 Artville, LLC, (all maps) iStockphoto.com/ © , p. 11 (peeler), p. 45 (pita); ©Clipart.com, pp. 8, 9; ©Debbie Walsh/maplespice.com, pp. 14, 17, 20, 23, 26, 29, 32, 35, 38, 41, 44; ©sf_foodphoto, p. 24 (piecrust); ©Jim Scherer Photography Inc./StockFood, p. 29 (soup); iStockphoto.com/© , p. 38 (pea soup) ;©Madeleine & Clancy Philippe, p. 32 (rougaille); ©Nayna Kanabar/simplysensationalfood.blogspot.com(sabji), p.14; ©Nicole DiMella/Enslow Publishers, Inc., p. 20 (poblanos), p. 22 (poblanos in pan), p. 26 (peanut stew); ©Pepy Nasution/indonesia-eats.blogspot.com, p. 41 (gado gado); ©Photoalto/Photolibrary, p. 7; ©Treloar-StockFood Munich/StockFood (cabbage pie), p. 23; United States Department of Agriculture (USDA), p. 12

Cover Illustration: © 2011 Photos.com, a division of Getty Images. All rights reserved.

Warning: The recipes in this book contain ingredients to which people may be allergic, such as peanuts and milk.

Contents

Introduction 4
Cooking Techniques 6
Cooking Terms 8
Cooking Tools 10
Nutrition 12
Conversions 13

1 Sabji (India) 14

2 Tofu (China) 17

3 Chiles Rellenos (Honduras) 20

4 Cabbage Pie (Russia) 23

5 Spinach Peanut Stew (Mali and Mauritania) 26

6 Mushroom Barley Soup (Tibet) 29

7 Tomatoes Rougaille (Mauritius) 32

8 Asparagus Frittata (Italy) 35

9 Pea Soup and Doughboys (Newfoundland) 38

10 Gado-Gado (Indonesia) 41

11 Falafel (Israel) 44

Further Reading 47
Internet Addresses 47
Index 48

Introduction

You have probably already eaten lots of vegetarian meals. Macaroni and cheese, potato soup, salads and peanut butter and jelly sandwiches are all meatless.

Vegetarians do not eat meat, poultry, or fish. Vegetarians do eat animal products such as milk, yogurt, cheese, butter, and eggs. A vegetarian diet is filled with vegetables, fruits, grains like rice, barley, and oats, and proteins like tofu, eggs, dried beans, and cheese. Vegans (*VEE-guns*) follow a more strict vegetarianism. They do not eat any animal products at all.

People choose vegetarian meals because they can be economical (cheaper). Othes do not believe in harming animals. Other people feel healthier eating little or no meat.

Vegetarians must get important nutrients like protein, iron, and calcium from other sources. Proteins (help your muscles) can be found in nuts and legumes—almonds, walnuts, cashews, peanuts, etc.; seeds—sunflower seeds, sesame seeds, pumpkin seeds, etc.; and dried beans—lentils, chickpeas, kidney beans, navy beans, split peas, etc. Iron (keeps blood healthy) can be found in dried fruits, baked beans, spinach, and tofu. Calcium (for strong bones and teeth) can be found in tofu, soy milk, milk, cheese, yogurt, collard greens, and molasses.

Each recipe in this book has specific directions on **WHAT YOU NEED** and **WHAT TO DO.** You will also find cooking tips. The tips help you to be safe and have fun in the kitchen. They will make you a more skillful chef.

Be Safe!

Whenever you are in the kitchen, there are important safety rules to follow.

1. Always **ask a responsible adult** for permission to cook. Always **have an adult** by your side when you use the oven, the stove, knives, or any appliance.

2. If you have long hair, tie it back. Remove dangling jewelry and tuck in any loose clothing.

3. Always use pot holders or oven mitts when handling anything on the stove or in the oven.

4. Never rush while cutting ingredients. You don't want the knife to slip.

5. If you are cooking something in the oven, stay in the house. Always use a timer—and stay where you can hear it.

6. If you are cooking something on the stove, stay in the kitchen.

7. ALLERGY ALERT! If you are cooking for someone else, let him or her know what ingredients you are using. Some people have life-threatening allergies to such foods as peanuts and shellfish.

Cooking Tips and Tricks

Keeping Clean:

- Wash your hands before you start. Make sure to also wash your hands after touching raw poultry, meat, or seafood and cracking eggs. These ingredients may have harmful germs that can make you very sick. Wash knives and cutting boards with soap and water after they've touched these ingredients.

- Use two cutting boards (one for meat and one for everything else) to avoid getting any germs from the meat on other food.

- Rinse all fruits and vegetables under cool water before you use them.

- Make sure your work space is clean before you start.

- Clean up as you cook.

Planning Ahead:

- Read the recipe from beginning to end before you start cooking. Make sure that you have all the ingredients and tools you will need before you start.

- If you don't understand something in a recipe, ask an adult for help.

Measuring:

- To measure dry ingredients, such as flour and sugar, dip the correct-size measuring cup into the ingredient until it is full. Then level off the top of the cup with the flat side of a butter knife. Brown sugar is the only dry ingredient that should be tightly packed into a measuring cup.

- To measure liquid ingredients, such as milk and oil, use a clear glass or plastic measuring cup. Make sure it is on a flat surface. Pour the liquid into the cup until it reaches the correct level. Check the measurement at eye level.

- Remember that measuring spoons come in different sizes. Be sure you are using a *teaspoon* if the recipe asks for it and not a *tablespoon*.

Mixing:

- Beat—Mix ingredients together *fast* with a wooden spoon, whisk, or an electric mixer.

- Mix—Blend ingredients together with a wooden spoon, an electric mixer, or a whisk.

- Stir—Combine ingredients using a wooden or metal spoon.

Cooking Terms

Cooking has its own vocabulary. Here are some terms you should be familiar with.

brown (verb)—To cook, usually in oil, until the food turns light brown.

chop—To cut into bite-sized pieces.

condiments—Foods that add a flavorful accent to a dish, such as ketchup, relish, and mustard.

Creole—A spicy sauce or dish made with tomatoes, peppers, onions, celery, and seasonings, and often served with rice.

cube—To cut into small cube-shaped pieces.

cuisine—The type of cooking used in a particular country.

dash (noun)—A very small amount, such as one shake of a salt shaker.

dice—To cut into small pieces (smaller than chopped), about ¼-inch sizes.

drizzle—To pour a small amount of liquid in a stream over a dish.

fry—To cook in hot fat in a pan on top of the stove.

garnish—A bit of colorful food, such as parsley, that adds flavor to a dish and makes it look more attractive.

herbs—Flowering plants used to give food a distinctive flavor, such as oregano, marjoram, parsley, and basil. They can be used fresh or dried.

mince—To chop into tiny pieces.

sauté—To fry lightly in oil or butter.

savory—Very flavorful but not sweet.

seasonings—Ingredients, such as salt, pepper, herbs and spices, used to bring out the flavor of a food.

simmer—To cook over low heat just below the boiling point.

spice—A seasoning that has a strong or spicy aroma, for example, cinnamon or pepper.

whisk (verb)—To beat quickly with a fork or wire whisk.

Cooking Tools

baking dish

cutting board

cookie sheet

frying pan

colander

mini muffin tins

measuring cups

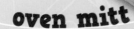
oven mitt

measuring spoons

pie pan

potato masher

paring knife

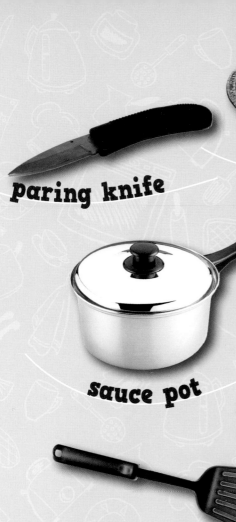
sauce pot

soup pot

spatula

tongs

whisk

wooden spoon

vegetable peeler

11

Nutrition

The best food is healthy as well as delicious. In planning meals, keep in mind the guidelines of the food pyramid.

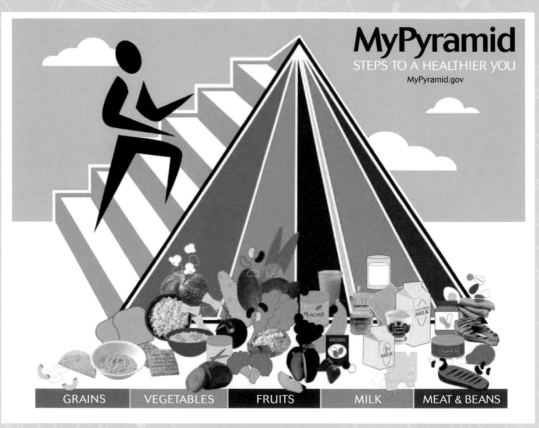

MyPyramid
STEPS TO A HEALTHIER YOU
MyPyramid.gov

GRAINS · VEGETABLES · FRUITS · MILK · MEAT & BEANS

GRAINS Make half your grains whole	VEGETABLES Vary your veggies	FRUITS Focus on fruits	MILK Get your calcium-rich foods	MEAT & BEANS Go lean with protein
Eat at least 3 oz. of whole-grain cereals, breads, crackers, rice, or pasta every day 1 oz. is about 1 slice of bread, about 1 cup of breakfast cereal, or 1/2 cup of cooked rice, cereal, or pasta	Eat more dark-green veggies like broccoli, spinach, and other dark leafy greens Eat more orange vegetables like carrots and sweet potatoes Eat more dry beans and peas like pinto beans, kidney beans, and lentils	Eat a variety of fruit Choose fresh, frozen, canned, or dried fruit Go easy on fruit juices	Go low-fat or fat-free when you choose milk, yogurt, and other milk products If you don't or can't consume milk, choose lactose-free products or other calcium sources such as fortified foods and beverages	Choose low-fat or lean meats and poultry Bake it, broil it, or grill it Vary your protein routine — choose more fish, beans, peas, nuts, and seeds

For a 2,000-calorie diet, you need the amounts below from each food group. To find the amounts that are right for you, go to MyPyramid.gov.

Eat 6 oz. every day	Eat 2 1/2 cups every day	Eat 2 cups every day	Get 3 cups every day; for kids aged 2 to 8, it's 2	Eat 5 1/2 oz. every day

Conversions

Recipes list amounts needed. Sometimes you need to know what that amount equals in another measurement. And sometimes you may want to make twice as much (or half as much) as the recipe yields. This chart will help you.

DRY INGREDIENT MEASUREMENTS	
Measure	**Equivalent**
1 tablespoon	3 teaspoons
¼ cup	4 tablespoons
½ cup	8 tablespoons
1 cup	16 tablespoons
2 cups	1 pound
½ stick of butter	¼ cup
1 stick of butter	½ cup
2 sticks of butter	1 cup
LIQUID INGREDIENT MEASUREMENTS	
8 fluid ounces	1 cup
1 pint (16 ounces)	2 cups
1 quart (2 pints)	4 cups
1 gallon (4 quarts)	16 cups

This book does not use abbreviations for measurements, but many cookbooks do. Here's what they mean.

c—cup

oz.—ounce

lb.—pound

T or tbsp.—tablespoon

t or tsp.—teaspoon

Chapter 1

Sabji

Sabji (*SUB-jee*) means "spicy vegetable dish" in Hindi, one of the main languages spoken in India. There are many sabji recipes. This one uses kidney beans, onions, potatoes, and Indian spices. It is cooked on top of the stove.

India

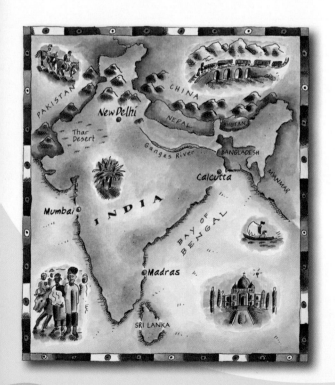

India is just a little bigger than Argentina, and about one-third the size of the United States. But it is the second most populated country in the world (behind China), with over one billion people.

In many homes, family members sit cross-legged on the floor for meals. They use plates made of banana leaves and eat food with their fingers.

Masala

Spices are very important in Indian cooking. The word *masala* means spices. Some of these spices are black pepper, cardamom, cinnamon, cloves, coriander, nutmeg, and turmeric.

What You Need

Equipment:
Soup pot

Frying pan with lid

Spatula or wooden spoon

Cutting board

Sharp knife

Colander

Ingredients:
2–3 medium white or Russet potatoes

1 8-ounce can kidney beans, rinsed

2 tablespoons vegetable oil or olive oil

1 medium yellow onion

1 tomato

1 cup frozen green peas

1 teaspoon salt

Fresh ground black pepper

Masala (Indian spices):
1 teaspoon curry powder

1 teaspoon turmeric

¼ teaspoon cayenne or chili powder

1 teaspoon ginger powder

½ teaspoon cumin

Cook's Tip

Instead of dry spices, buy a jar of Indian sauce, like tandoori paste, from the grocery store. Stir ¼ cup or more into your sabji.

What to Do

1. Measure, scrub, and cube the potatoes. Put them in a soup pot and cover with water.
2. Boil potatoes until soft. This takes about 15–20 minutes. Drain.
3. Dice the onion.
4. Heat oil in frying pan.
5. Sauté onions in oil until translucent, about 3–4 minutes.
6. Dice tomato. Add to onions and stir.
7. Add all spices. Stir.
8. Drain and rinse the kidney beans.
9. Add beans, cooked potatoes, and frozen peas to the pan. Stir.
10. Cover pan with lid and simmer until heated, about 5–10 minutes, stirring occasionally.

Serves 3–4.

What's This?

Pour potatoes into a colander to pour off the liquid. Careful! It's hot.

What's This?

Soft and almost see-through.

Cook's Tip

Sauté means to fry lightly in oil or butter.

Cook's Tip

If your sabji seems too dry, add ¼ cup of water.

Did You Know?

Beans are a good source of protein.

Chapter 2
Tofu

Tofu (*TOE-foo*) is bean curd made from soybeans. Tofu is rich in protein and iron. It is soft and bland (has little flavor). But it absorbs flavor like a sponge. Tofu is good fried, baked, steamed, or raw. Seasoned tofu is good in soups, salads, and sandwiches.

China

China is a huge country on the continent of Asia. It has the world's largest country in population and the third largest in area. About a fifth of the world's people live in China.

In ancient China, five sacred grains (*wu ku*) were essential for life: soybeans, rice, wheat, barley, and millet.

Soy Sauce

Soy sauce is made from fermented soybeans, roasted grain, water, and salt. Soy sauce was invented in China almost 2,500 years ago. Soy sauce is a poplar condiment used to flavor many Asian foods.

What's This?
Fermentation is a chemical process that causes bubbles of gas to form.

What You Need

Equipment:
Sharp knife

Cutting board

Fork

Measuring spoons

Frying pan with lid

Spatula

Ingredients:
Tofu

Cabbage (optional)

Spinach (optional)

For Marinade:
3 tablespoons soy sauce

3 tablespoons vegetable oil

2 teaspoons rice or cider vinegar

1 teaspoon fresh ginger root, grated

2 fresh scallions (green onions) diced

1 teaspoon sesame oil

1 clove garlic, minced

ground black pepper

hot pepper flakes

What's This?
Marinade is flavorful liquid. When food soaks in a marinade (or marinates), it absorbs the flavor.

What's This?
A clove is one section of a garlic bulb. Take the papery skin off before using it.

What to Do

1. Slice tofu into ½-inch slices.

2. Mix marinade ingredients in a bowl. Whisk with a fork.

3. Combine marinade and tofu. Let it sit for 15 minutes.

4. Cook tofu.

   <u>For soft tofu:</u> Place tofu and marinade in the frying pan. Cover and simmer over medium to low heat for 5 minutes.

   <u>For crispy tofu:</u> Heat 1 tablespoon of oil in frying pan. Lift tofu from the marinade. Pat dry and coat with cornstarch. Brown tofu slices about 2–3 minutes on each side in the uncovered frying pan.

5. Flip the tofu with a spatula or tongs.

6. Add chopped cabbage or spinach to the pan if desired.

7. Simmer and stir for 5 more minutes. Serve tofu with warm cooked rice and a side of vegetables.

Serves 3–4.

Cook's Tip

The oil, soy sauce, and vinegar are important to the marinade, but all the other ingredients are optional. Add only the ones you like!

Chapter 3

Chiles Rellenos

In Spanish, the word *relleno* means "stuffed." Chiles are peppers. This recipe for stuffed peppers is baked. But chiles rellenos (*CHEE-lays ray-YAY-nose*) are often fried.

Honduras

Honduras is in Central America. The country's landscape goes from mountains to jungle to coast on the Caribbean Sea.

Honduras's national bird is the scarlet macaw. The bird can live for 50 years in the wild.

Poblano Peppers

The poblano (*poe-BLAH-no*) is like a green pepper. It is a darker color. In peppers, much of the spicy heat comes from the seeds. The outer skin is tough. Cooks remove the seeds and skin before cooking.

What You Need

Equipment:

Baking dish

Cutting board

Grater

Bowl

Fork or whisk

Ingredients:

6 poblano peppers, canned, jarred, or freshly roasted

½ pound Monterey Jack cheese

1 teaspoon cumin

3 eggs

½ cup milk

1 teaspoon salt

½ teaspoon pepper

What's This?

To roast fresh peppers:

Slice peppers down one side. Remove seeds. Rinse.

Broil on a baking sheet, about 5 minutes on each side. The skin will burn.

With tongs, place peppers in a brown paper bag. Close the top so the peppers steam.

Wait 15–30 minutes. When peppers are cool, peel off the skin.

What to Do

1. Preheat oven to 350 degrees.
2. Grease the baking dish with oil, butter, or spray-on cooking oil.
3. Grate the cheese.
4. Place peppers side by side in a baking dish. Fill peppers with cheese.
5. Crack the eggs into a bowl. Add milk, cumin, salt, and pepper. Beat with a fork or whisk.
6. Pour the batter over peppers.
7. Bake uncovered for 25 minutes, until the eggs are set.

Serves 5–6.

Use your fingers or a piece of waxed paper to spread the grease around.

The poblanos in the batter shouldn't jiggle.

Chapter 4

Cabbage Pie

Russia is a northern country. Russian food must keep people warm during long, cold winters. This pie is filled with cabbage, cheese, and eggs. It is delicious, warm, and comforting.

Russia

Moscow, Russia's capital, is the largest city in the world, not by population but by size. It is over 9,000 square miles.

The land region of Siberia makes up 77 percent of Russia's land. Few people live in Siberia. The country has cold subarctic temperatures, from 5 to 32 °F in January and about 68°F in July.

Pie

Pie is not only for dessert. For main meals, a savory double-crust pie is also called "potpie." Mashed potatoes are the top crust for shepherd's pie. A quiche (*keesh*) is a single-crust pie made with vegetables, cheese, and eggs.

What You Need

Equipment:

Pie pan

Cutting board

Sharp knife

Butter knife

Frying pan

Spatula

Ingredients:

2 ready-made piecrusts

1 small head of green cabbage

½ pound mushrooms

1 small yellow onion

3 tablespoons butter

1 teaspoon salt

½ teaspoon pepper

½ teaspoon basil

½ teaspoon marjoram

½ teaspoon tarragon

4 ounces cream cheese, softened (left out of the refrigerator until it reaches room temperature)

4 to 5 hard-boiled eggs

1 tablespoon fresh dill weed, finely chopped

Cook's Tip

Pie crusts are available at the grocery store in the freezer or dairy aisle.

What's This?

Dill is a tangy herb. If you don't have fresh dill, use 1 teaspoon of dried dill.

What to Do

1. Shred the cabbage. Dice the onion. Slice the mushrooms.

2. Melt butter in frying pan.

3. Sauté vegetables for 3–5 minutes.

4. Add salt, pepper, and herbs (except dill). Stir. Turn off the heat.

5. Peel and slice hard-boiled eggs.

6. Place the bottom piecrust in the pie pan. Fill the pie: Spread the cream cheese on the bottom. Place the egg slices on top of the cream cheese. Sprinkle the dill on top of the eggs. Add the sautéed vegetables.

7. Place the top crust over the pie. To trim, cut off the extra crust with a knife. The crust should be the same size as the pie pan. If any crust hangs over the edge, trim it off with a knife.

8. Crimp the piecrust edges. Make slices in top crust. (Slices let steam escape during baking.)

9. Bake at 400°F (205°C) for 15 minutes. Turn oven down to 350°F (180°C). Bake 20 to 25 minutes longer, until the pie is golden.

What's This?

To crimp, press crusts together with a fork or your fingers. This makes a seal to keep juices inside the pie.

Cook's Tip

Clean mushrooms by brushing the dirt off with a soft brush or paper towel or by washing gently. Cut off the very bottom of the stem and throw it away, then use the rest.

Cook's Tip

To hard-boil eggs, place in cold water. Turn heat onto high and boil for 2 minutes. Turn off heat. Let eggs sit in the hot water for 10 minutes. Place in cold water to cool.

Peeling an egg is easier if you hit the eggshell gently on the counter to crack it all over, then peel off the shell under running water.

25

Chapter 5

Spinach Peanut Stew

Peanut butter makes this stew creamy and rich. In Mali and Mauritania, many dishes are flavored with peanuts. Peanuts are a good source of protein.

Mali and Mauritania

Mali and Mauritania are in northwest Africa. The Sahara Desert covers most of the region. Drought is common. Water is scarce. Peanut crops are watered by the Niger River, which runs through both countries.

Onions

Onions have a strong flavor and odor. They can irritate your eyes enough to make you cry when you cut them. But they become mild and mellow when cooked.

What You Need

Equipment:

Cutting board

Sharp knife

Skillet or frying pan

Wooden spoon or spatula

Hot pad

Ingredients:

1 tablespoon vegetable oil or olive oil

1 medium onion

½ teaspoon salt

¼ teaspoon black pepper

2 tablespoons peanut butter (creamy or crunchy)

3 tablespoons tomato paste

1 tomato

3 cups chopped fresh spinach OR 1 package frozen spinach, thawed

¼–½ cup chopped peanuts

Dash of cayenne pepper

½ cup water or vegetable stock

What to Do

1. Dice the onion and tomato.
2. Pour oil into frying pan. Heat over medium heat.
3. Add onion. Add salt and pepper. Sauté for 2–3 minutes.
4. Stir in peanut butter, tomato paste, and tomato.
5. Add a dash of cayenne pepper.
6. Add spinach and peanuts. Stir.

Cook's Tip

Slice and peel off the papery covering of the onion, then slice the white layers.

What's This?

Dried chili pepper. It's spicy hot!

7. Add water or stock.
8. Cover and simmer, stirring occasionally, for 10–15 minutes.

Serve the hot stew over rice. (Cook the rice according to directions on the package.)

Serves 5–6.

Chapter 6
Mushroom Barley Soup

Barley is a grain. It is a little chewy, like brown rice. The barley plant can thrive in poor soil. Barley is a staple food in Tibet. Tibetans grind barley flour to make a hot cereal called tsampa.

Tibet

Tibet sits between Nepal, India, and China. Some people call Tibet "the roof of the world." The world's tallest mountain range, the Himalayas, including Mount Everest, borders southern Tibet. Lhasa, Tibet's capital, has the highest elevation of any capital in the world. Its altitude is 11,450 feet.

Yak Butter

Yaks are long-haired animals related to cows. Yaks live in the Himalayas. They thrive in high mountains. Tibetans herd yaks for milk and butter. Yak butter is a very important food in Tibet. People also spin yak hair into yarn.

What You Need

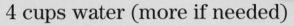

Equipment:
Cutting board
Sharp knife
Large soup pan
Mixing spoon
Hot pad

Ingredients:
½ cup raw, uncooked barley
4 cups water (more if needed)
1 pound mushrooms
1 large onion
3 tablespoons butter
1 teaspoon salt
2–3 tablespoons soy sauce
Freshly ground black pepper

Cook's Tip

Use cow's milk butter! You probably won't find yak butter.

Cook's Tip

Grinding peppercorns releases the peppery flavor.

What to Do

1. In the soup pan, cook the barley in the water. It may take 30–40 minutes or so.

2. While the barley cooks, chop the onion. Slice the mushrooms until you have about 2 cups.

3. In a frying pan, melt butter over medium heat.

4. Put the mushrooms and onion and salt in the pan. Sauté until soft.

5. When the barley is tender, scoop the mushrooms and onions with a spatula into the soup.

6. Stir in soy sauce and pepper. Simmer over very low heat for about 15 minutes.

Cook's Tip

Mushrooms shrink and release water as they cook. Keep the mushroom liquid in the pan. It is rich and flavorful.

The soup should be thick. The barley grains should be tender and a little chewy. You can add a dab of butter if you want.

One recipe describes barley soup this way: "There will be a golden sheen on the surface and the heavenly smell will waft you across the Himalayas."

Serves 4–6.

Chapter 7

Tomatoes Rougaille

The word rougaille (*roo-GAHY*) refers to Creole spices, like thyme and ginger. The cooks of Mauritius borrow flavors from Indian, Chinese, and French dishes. The best part about this recipe is that you don't have to cook it! Just mix it in a bowl and pour it over warm cooked rice.

Mauritius

Mauritius is an island nation in the Indian Ocean. Its chief island, also called Mauritius, lies about 500 miles east of Madagascar and about 2,450 miles southwest of India.

Mauritius is the only known home of the dodo. The bird was first seen by Europeans in 1600. The dodo became extinct less than eighty years later.

Tomatoes

In Creole cooking, tomatoes are called "pommes d'amour," a French phrase meaning "apples of love." Tomatoes rougaille is often used as a chutney, a sauce or relish with sweet and tangy flavors.

What You Need

Equipment:
Cutting board
Sharp knife
Mixing spoon
Bowl

Cook's *Tip*

Use a sweet onion like red or Vidalia.

Ingredients:
1 green pepper
1 medium onion
1½–2 cups tomatoes, fresh or canned

Cook's *Tip*

Dice 3 fresh tomatoes, or use a 12–16-ounce can of diced tomatoes (including the juice).

Seasonings:

1 clove minced garlic

½ teaspoon dry ginger OR minced fresh ginger root

½ teaspoon dried coriander OR 2 tablespoons freshly minced coriander or parsley

A dash of cayenne or hot pepper sauce (like Tabasco)

½ teaspoon salt, to taste

Fresh ground pepper, to taste

Rice (cook following the directions on the package)

Cook's Tip

As in most recipes, experiment with spices. Use only the ones you like.

What's This?

Coriander is an herb used a lot in Indian and Middle Eastern foods. It is also known as cilantro.

What to Do

1. Finely dice green pepper and onion.
2. Dice tomatoes or open the can.
3. Mix all ingredients (except rice) in bowl.
4. Serve tomatoes rougaille cold or room temperature. Pour over bowls of warm rice.

Serves 3-4.

What's This?

Finely means very small pieces.

Chapter 8

Asparagus Frittata

A frittata is an Italian omelette. It is made with eggs, vegetables, and cheese. You can start a frittata cooking on the stove and you can finish cooking it under the oven's broiler.

Italy

Food is important in Italian culture. In Italy, people can spend two or three hours at the main meal, relaxing with family and friends. Favorite Italian foods are spaghetti, lasagna, and pizza.

Asparagus

Asparagus is a delicacy for many chefs. Stalks picked in early spring are tender. Asparagus is a perennial; it comes up every year. Asparagus can grow wild, even along railroad tracks and highways.

What You Need

Equipment:
Cutting board
Sharp knife
Bowl
Whisk
Spatula
Frying pan with lid
Soup Pot

Ingredients:
½ pound fresh asparagus
2 tablespoons olive oil
1 small onion
1 clove garlic
6 eggs
Salt
Pepper
½ cup grated Parmesan or cheddar cheese

Cook's Tip

You can also make this frittata with broccoli, zucchini, mushrooms, or spinach. Sauté the raw vegetables with the onion.

What to Do

1. Rinse asparagus. Snap off the bottom ends.

2. Cut asparagus spears into ½-inch pieces.

3. Place asparagus in a soup pan with an inch of water. Simmer just until tender, only about 1 or 2 minutes. Drain the water. Set the asparagus aside.

4. Chop the onion. Mince the garlic.

5. Crack eggs into a bowl. Beat the eggs with a fork or whisk until frothy.

6. Heat oil in a frying pan over medium heat.

7. Sauté onion for 5 minutes. Add garlic and asparagus and cook for one more minute.

8. Pour beaten eggs over vegetables in the frying pan.

9. Reduce heat to medium low. Cover. Cook for about 5–6 minutes.

10. Turn off heat. Lift the lid. Sprinkle cheese on top. Cover to let the cheese melt.

11. Slice the frittata and serve hot.

Serves 4–5.

The ends of asparagus are "woody" and tough. Bend the stalk near the bottom until an inch or two snaps off. Throw that part away.

Jiggle the pan. If the eggs wiggle, they need to cook a little longer.

Chapter 9

Pea Soup and Doughboys

Pea soup and Doughboys is soup, with floating dumplings, or steamed biscuits.

Newfoundland

Newfoundland is an island in the Atlantic Ocean. It is part of Canada. Its largest city is St. John's, with a population of just over 100,000.

Newfoundland is the easternmost point in North America. Some icebergs that break off Greenland's coast drift past Newfoundland.

Dumplings

Dumplings are cooked balls of dough. They are like soft biscuits. They are cooked right in the soup or stew.

What You Need

Equipment:

Large saucepan

Sharp knife

Cutting board

Stirring spoon

Bowl

Measuring cups and spoons

Ingredients:

Soup:

1 cup yellow split peas

3 cups water

1 medium onion

1 stalk celery

2 waxy potatoes (try using small red potatoes)

1 carrot

2 dried bay leaves

1 teaspoon sea salt

Black pepper

Dumplings:

½ cup all purpose flour

½ teaspoon salt

2 teaspoons baking powder

½ teaspoon mixed herbs (such as parsley or chives)

4 tablespoons butter

½ to 1 cup cold water or milk

What's This?

Bay leaves come from the laurel tree. Simmered in soup, whole bay leaves add flavor.

What to Do

Soup:

1. Rinse the peas. Put peas in a saucepan with 3 cups water and the bay leaves.
3. Bring to a boil. Boil for 10 minutes. Reduce to low and simmer for 1 hour. Stir now and then.
4. While the peas cook, dice the onion, celery, carrots, and potatoes.
5. Mash peas with a potato masher.
6. Stir in the sea salt and black pepper.
7. Add the vegetables. Stir the soup. Bring back to a boil. Then simmer for 20 more minutes. Stir often so it doesn't burn.
8. If you wish add more water to thin soup.
9. While soup is cooking, make the dumpling dough.

Cook's Tip

When the soup is done, take out the bay leaves!

Dumplings:

1. In a bowl, mix all the dry ingredients.
2. With a dull knife, slice the butter into small pieces. Add to the dry ingredients, mashing with a fork until the butter is blended.
3. Add water or milk. Stir with a wooden spoon until the dough forms. Adjust the amount until you have a moist dumpling dough.
4. With a spoon, scoop up balls of dough. Drop them into the soup. Cover and simmer for 10–15 minutes, until the doughboys are puffed up and cooked.
5. Stir now and then to make sure the dumplings don't stick.

Serves 4.

Chapter 10

Gado-Gado

"Gado-gado" means "mix-mix." In Indonesia, this salad is a complete one-dish meal. The word for sauce is *bumbu*. Gado-gado uses peanut bumbu.

Indonesia

Indonesia is the world's largest archipelago (*ar-kih-PEL-uh-go*), or chain of islands. Indonesia is made of 17,000 islands. The capital city is Jakarta, on the island of Java.

Indonesia

What You Need

Equipment:
Colander

Cutting board

Sharp knife

Saucepan

Stirring spoon

Large bowl

Small bowl or jar with lid (to mix dressing)

Ingredients:
Vegetables:

1 potato

1 cup cabbage, shredded

2 cups green beans

2 medium carrots, peeled and sliced thinly

1 cup cauliflower florets

Water

Dressing:
½ cup crunchy peanut butter

¼ cup hot water

½ cup vegetable oil

2 cloves garlic, chopped

4 shallots, chopped

¼ teaspoon salt

½ teaspoon hot sauce OR ¼ teaspoon cayenne pepper

½ teaspoon brown sugar

1 tablespoon soy sauce

1 tablespoon lemon juice OR apple cider vinegar

Garnish:
1 cup bean sprouts, washed lettuce

2 or 3 hard-boiled eggs

Tomato

Cucumber

Peanuts (optional)

What to Do

1. Chop the vegetables into small pieces.

2. Boil the potatoes in water in a saucepan until tender, 10 minutes.

3. Boil the rest of the vegetables in water with 1 teaspoon salt, for 2–4 minutes.

4. Strain the vegetables in a colander to drain all the water.

5. Boil the eggs for 2–3 minutes. Keep them in the hot water for ten minutes. Cool, peel, and slice the eggs.

6. Arrange a layer of lettuce in a serving bowl or platter.

7. Make the dressing. Dissolve peanut butter in hot water. Add remaining ingredients. Mix. Adjust amounts to your taste. Like it tangier? Add another tablespoon of lemon or vinegar. Want it thicker? Add more peanut butter. Saltier? More soy sauce. Spicier? Another dash of hot sauce or chili powder.

8. Scoop the vegetables onto the lettuce. Add tomatoes and cucumber.

9. Pour the dressing over the salad. (Gado-gado is good warm or cold. Store leftover dressing in the refrigerator.)

10. Top with bean sprouts and sliced eggs or peanuts.

Serves 2–4.

Cook's Tip

Try slicing the carrots at an angle.

Cook's Tip

Other veggie cooking options include frying, steaming, or using raw.

Cook's Tip

Mix dressing in a jar. Put the lid on tight. Shake it up!

Chapter 11

Falafel

Falafel (*fuh-LA-ful*) is fried or baked balls of chickpea dough. Falafel is a popular food across the Middle East.

Tahini is like peanut butter made from sesame seeds. It is creamy, oily, light colored, and delicious. It is often an ingredient in Middle Eastern dishes.

Israel

Israel is a small country in southwestern Asia. The country occupies a narrow strip of land located on the eastern shore of the Mediterranean Sea. Israel was founded as a homeland for Jews from all parts of the world.

What You Need

Equipment:

Cutting board

Sharp knife

Mixing bowl

Fork, potato masher, or food processor

Mini-muffin tins (or cookie sheet or frying pan)

Ingredients:

1 15 oz. can chickpeas, drained

1 small onion, finely chopped

1 teaspoon minced garlic

2 tablespoons fresh parsley, finely chopped

Seasonings:

1 teaspoon coriander

¾ teaspoon cumin

¼ teaspoon turmeric

Dash of cayenne or chili powder

½ teaspoon salt

Fresh ground black pepper

2 tablespoons flour

1 teaspoon baking powder

1 tablespoon lemon juice

1 tablespoon olive oil

Optional: 1 tablespoon tahini

Cook's Tip

Tahini may have a layer of oil on top. Stir tahini before you use it.

For falafel sandwich:

Pita

Cucumber

Onion

Tomato

Creamy dressing or yogurt sauce

What's This?

Round flatbread. Slice the round in half down the middle. Each half will pop open and make a "pocket" for your sandwich.

What to Do

Make falafel:

1. Mash the first 4 ingredients together. Use a potato masher, fork, or food processor.
2. Mix in the seasonings.
3. With a fork or wooden spoon, stir in the rest of the ingredients.
4. Bake or fry.

To bake:

1. Preheat oven to 400°F degrees.
2. Option 1: Grease mini-muffin tins with oil or shortening, or spray-on cooking oil. Scoop dough in Ping-Pong-sized balls. Plop in muffin tins. Bake twenty minutes.
3. Option 2: Grease a cookie sheet. Flatten the balls into patties. Bake ten minutes. Flip. Bake ten more minutes.

To fry:

1. Heat a thin layer of oil in a frying pan. Fry falafel balls for a few minutes on each side until they have a crispy crust. Add more oil as needed.

Make a sandwich:

1. Pop hot falafel into pita.
2 Add sliced cucumbers and tomato and onion.
3. Pour on a creamy salad dressing OR plain yogurt mixed with a squirt of lemon juice and salt and pepper.

Serves 4.

Further Reading

Books

D'Amico, Joan, and Karen Eich Drummond. *The Coming to America Cookbook: Delicious Recipes and Fascinating Stories from America's Many Cultures.* Hoboken, N.J.: John Wiley & Sons, 2005.

De Mariaffi, Elisabeth. *Eat It Up! Lip-Smacking Recipes for Kids.* Toronto: Owlkids, 2009.

Dodge, Abigail Johnson. *Around the World Cookbook.* New York: DK Publishing, 2008.

Lagasse, Emeril. *Emeril's There's a Chef in My World!: Recipes That Take You Places.* New York: HarperCollins Publishers, 2006.

Wagner, Lisa. *Cool Sweets & Treats to Eat: Easy Recipes for Kids to Cook.* Edina, Minn.: ABDO Publishing Co., 2007.

Internet Addresses

Cookalotamus Kids

<http://www.cookalotamus.com/kids.html>

PBS Kids: Cafe Zoom

<http://pbskids.org/zoom/activities/cafe/>

Spatulatta.com

<http://www.spatulatta.com/>

Index

A

allergies, 5
asparagus, 36
asparagus frittata, 35–37

B

bay leaves, 39
beans, 16

C

cabbage pie, 23–25
cayenne pepper, 28
chiles rellenos, 20–22
China, 17, 18
chutney, 33
cilantro, 34
conversions, 13
cooking
    terms, 8–9, 16, 18
    tips, tricks, 6–7, 18, 25
    tools, 10–11
coriander, 34
crimping edges, 25

D

dill weed, 24
dumplings, 39, 40

E

eggs, peeling, 25

F

falafel, 44–46
fermentation, 18
food pyramid, 12

G

gado-gado, 41–43
garlic cloves, 18

H

Honduras, 20

I

India, 14
Indonesia, 41
Israel, 44
Italy, 35

M

Mali, Mauritania, 26
marinade, 18
masala, 15
Mauritius, 32
measuring, 7, 13
mixing, 7
mushroom barley soup,
    29–31
mushrooms, cleaning, 25

N

Newfoundland, 38
nutrition, 12

O

onions, 27

P

pea soup and
    doughboys, 38–40
pie, 24

pita, 45
poblano peppers, 21
potpie, 24

Q

quiche, 24

R

roasting peppers, 21
Russia, 23

S

sabji, 14–16
safety, 5
shepherd's pie, 24
Siberia, 23
soy sauce, 18
spices, 9, 15
spinach peanut stew,
    26–28
stuffed peppers, 20–22

T

tahini, 44
Tibet, 29
tofu, 17–19
tomatoes, 33
tomatoes rougaille,
    32–34

Y

yak butter, 30